The Essential Buyer's Guide

Porsche
987 BOXSTER
& CAYMAN

1st Generation. Model years 2005 to 2009 Boxster,
Boxster S, Boxster Spyder, Cayman & Cayman S

Your marque expert:
Adrian Streather

T0386759

VELOCE PUBLISHING
THE PUBLISHER OF FINE AUTOMOTIVE BOOKS

www.veloce.co.uk

For post publication news, updates and amendments relating to this book please visit www.veloce.co.uk/books/V4424

First published in September 2012 by Veloce Publishing Limited, Veloce House, Parkway Farm Business Park, Middle Farm Way, Poundbury, Dorchester DT1 3AR, England. Fax 01305 268864 / e-mail info@veloce.co.uk / web www.veloce.co.uk or www.velocebooks.com. Reprinted April 2016. ISBN: 978-1-845844-24-0 UPC: 6-36847-04424-4.

Introduction
– the purpose of this book

The information in this buyer's guide is arranged in user-friendly chapters to allow any prospective purchaser of a road legal 1st generation Porsche 987 series Boxster or Cayman model to make informed decisions on whether or not to proceed, with a purchase after viewing and test driving a specific car.

Anyone considering purchasing a 1st generation 987 Boxster or Cayman should be aware that they are getting into newer models with significantly higher prices than the previous 986 Boxster model range. In other words, a second-hand 1st generation 987 series Boxster or Cayman is going to be quite expensive.

The 987 Cayman is essentially a hatchback version (Coupé with rear hatch) of the Boxster, and represents Porsche AG's re-entry into the 'hot hatch' business: its last being the Porsche 968 launched in the early 1990s. Sadly, the 968 was not a sales success, although the 1st generation 987 Boxster and the 987 Cayman series started with impressive yearly production numbers and worldwide sales, the world financial meltdown in 2008 reduced production of the entire 987 series by around 50%, and it was replaced by the 2nd generation 987 series in model year 2009. Also by this time it had become apparent that Porsche AG had fallen back into its old 1980s way of thinking. The company not only built the standard 987 models, consisting of the Boxster, Boxster S, Cayman and Cayman S, but also started to produce low numbers of 'special edition models', such as the Boxster Orange, Boxster and Boxster S Sport Editions, Boxster S Porsche Design Edition II, Cayman S Porsche Design Edition I, Cayman S Sport Edition, along with slightly larger numbers of the Boxster S RS 60 Spyder. As a result, sometimes it can be hard for the potential 1st generation 987 series purchaser to determine the originality of a specific car offered for sale, because the model on sale might look strange painted bright orange, but it is original. However, as always, the best advice is to take care, and always

The Porsche 968 was Porsche AG's last true 'hot hatch' before the 987 Cayman. (Author collection)

1st generation 987 Cayman S first rolled off the line in model year 2005. (Courtesy Porsche AG archive)

ask for the papers. The old adage 'show me the papers' still applies in the second decade of the 21st century when buying a used car.

The 1st generation of the 987 Boxster and Cayman model range started rolling off the production lines in Germany (Boxster and Cayman) and Finland (Boxster only) in model year 2005 and finished in model year 2009 when the 2nd generation 987 series went into full production. 1st and 2nd generation 987 models shared the production line from model year 2008, but production of the 1st generation was not terminated until part way into model year 2009 (run out models or country specific end of production specials). The total number of 1st generation Boxster models produced was 57,314, while there were a total of 44,660 1st generation 987 Cayman models.

Owning a pre-loved 1st generation 987 Boxster, Boxster S or Boxster R60 Spyder, Cayman, Cayman S, or one of the special edition models, can provide years of motoring pleasure and enjoyment through being part of the Porsche experience – albeit that the Porsche experience is now revolving around very complicated technology. There's very few Porsche models left that allow the DIY (do-it-yourself) car enthusiast to indulge in getting one's hands dirty in the garage.

Special thanks to all credited photographic contributors mentioned in this book, and to Laurance Yap of Porsche Cars Canada Ltd.

1st generation 987 Boxster was just as popular as its predecessor.
(Author collection)

The Essential Buyer's Guide™ currency
At the time of publication a BG unit of currency "●" equals approximately £1.00/US$1.43/Euro 1.28. Please adjust to suit current exchange rates using Sterling as the base currency.

Contents

1 Is it the right car for you?
– marriage guidance

Tall and short drivers
All 1st generation 987 Boxster and Cayman models in left– and right-hand drive configurations provide a comfortable driving position for short and tall drivers as an adjustable position steering wheel is installed.

Weight of controls
All 987 Boxster and Cayman models are fitted with power steering, which helps to significantly reduce loads on the arms. All are fitted with a very effective mechanical vacuum brake boost system. The hydraulic clutch operating system, fitted in conjunction with a manual transmission, is reasonably light and not so hard on the left leg.

Will it fit the garage?
Chapter 17 contains a table with specific model dimensions. Measure your garage, not forgetting that the doors (and the Cayman's hatchback) have to be opened in the garage.

Interior space
There's plenty of leg room in the 987 Boxster and Cayman models for both driver and passenger. Seat comfort does depend on type of seat installed. The standard comfort seat nicely supports people of average girth, but the optional sports seat is just that little bit more comfortable (big bit in author's opinion) as it grips ones hips.

Luggage capacity
The 987 Boxster and Boxster S models are two-seat Roadsters and have little room for anything, but two people and a few knick-knacks. However, because the engine is mounted in the middle these models have a front and rear luggage compartment, each capable of accommodating a suitcase. A little room is lost in the front luggage compartment because that's where the spare wheel and tyre assembly is installed. The 987 Cayman and Cayman S models, being mid-engined Coupés with a hatchback, are provided with the same size front luggage compartment as the Boxster models but have direct access from the passenger compartment as well as through the rear tailgate into a very spacious rear hatch compartment.

Running costs
Due to the relative newness of the 1st generation 987 Boxster and Cayman model ranges, the cost of ownership is higher than the previous 986 Boxster series in some areas, although, if the car's still under some form of warranty, unscheduled maintenance costs will be lower. However, the 987 Boxsters and Caymans are powerful sports cars designed to be driven hard, and the resulting cost of ownership is higher than for a standard road car.

Usability
It's a sports car and I do not recommend the 1st generation 987 Boxster and Cayman models be driven on snow- and ice-covered roads, even with proper winter

tyres, and any other installed safety systems such as Porsche Stability Management (PSM). The ride height is too low for harsh conditions, and salt used on snow and ice on the roads in winter will always find an area of bare metal to get its corrosive teeth into.

Parts availability
To date no issues related to parts availability have been reported for any of the 1st generation 987 series.

Parts cost
It's a Porsche sports car; expect parts to be relatively expensive.

Insurance
Check with your insurance company, as a Boxster or Cayman can be expensive to fully insure. If you cannot afford full insurance coverage, you shouldn't purchase one of these cars.

Investment potential
The 987 Boxster, followed by the 987 Cayman, offer good bang for your buck in the sports car market, but do not expect to make a profit on resale.

Foibles
Too much modern technology and ever-increasing weight. Carrying out DIY (home) repairs is very difficult, if not impossible. Workshop manual subscription from Porsche AG is very expensive.

Plus points
Every girl loves a Porsche, and in the case of the 987 Boxster, Boxster S, Cayman and Cayman S, it is love at first sight for many. The new 987 Cayman model range's hatchback offers an appealing mix of sports car one day, and other functions the next. In other words, very attractive to the female driver species. Reliable. Flexible.

Minus points
Purchase price. Myriad of variations available. Complicated technology, and is this desirable in a Porsche sports car? Navigation system can be expensive to upgrade.

Alternatives
Porsche 986 Boxster, Mazda MX-5 Miata, BMW Z3, BMW Z4, Honda S2000, Mercedes SLK.

The ladies love the 987 Cayman S, the newest hot hatch from Porsche AG. (Courtesy Porsche AG archive)

2 Cost considerations
– affordable, or a money pit

Service by an approved Porsche dealer
Intervals: 12,000 miles/20,000km (small) and 24,000 miles/40,000km (large) Small
service cost: from ●x299 Large service cost: from ●x600

Mechanical parts cost
Rebuilt 2.7-litre M97.20 engine: from ●x5250
Rebuilt 3.2-litre M97.26 engine: from ●x6250
Rebuilt 3.4-litre M97.21 engine: from ●x7250
Rebuilt G87.01 manual transmission: from ●x3500
Rebuilt A87.20 Tiptronic transmission: from ●x4000
Radiator (from 997): from ●x238 each
Clutch kit: from ●x275 (kit and fitting by Porsche dealer from ●x1400)
Steel cross-drilled brake discs (rotors) front (pair): ●x362
Steel cross-drilled brake discs (rotors) rear (pair): ●x386
Brake pads front (pair): ●x90
Brake pads rear (pair): ●x125
ABS hydraulic unit: ●x2025
Front windscreen (windshield) wiper arm assemblies (pair): ●x67
Front wiper blades (pair): ●x22

Electronic and electrical parts cost
Alternator: from ●x350
ABS control unit (all): from ●x1132
Heating and air-conditioning control unit: ●x161
Engine control unit (DME) for all engine capacities and types: ●x2862
Porsche Communication Management 2.1 system: from ●x4000
Porsche Communication Management 2.1 control head: from ●x1299
Porsche Communication Management 2.1 Navigation DVD unit: from ●x599
Porsche Communication Management 2.1 Navigation updates: from ●x299
Window electric motor: ●x155
Rear spoiler drive motor: ●x692
Headlight: from ●x160
Battery (80 amp/hr): ●x133

Structural work cost
LHD to RHD conversion: Don't even consider it!
Complete body restoration: from ●x15,000
New body shell: Price on application from local Porsche dealer
Full repaint (including preparation): from ●x5000
Full professional restoration from basket case: from ●x25,000

Manuals
Factory workshop manual set: from ●x5200
Original 987 Boxster or Cayman owner's manual set: ●x200

Parts that are easy to find
All 987 Boxster and Cayman parts are easily obtained from your local factory-approved dealer or independent Porsche parts supplier.

Parts that are hard to find
No shortages of 1st generation 987 Boxster or Cayman parts have been reported.

Parts that are very expensive
- Litronic headlight system.
- Porsche Ceramic Composite Brake (PCCB) discs (rotors) and pads.
- Fabric for rag top (convertible).

Simple DIY servicing reduces 987 ownership costs considerably. (Courtesy Russ Standage)

All parts for the 1st generation 987 Cayman S are easily obtained. (Author collection)

Sports Chrono interior. (Courtesy Porsche AG archive)

3 Living with a 987
– will you get along together?

Purchasing any Porsche model is going to have an impact on your entire family and, like its ancestors, the 987 Boxster or Cayman models are not practical or family cars. Both types were designed for high-speed driving through the Swiss Alps or hurtling down the German autobahn, French autoroute, Italian autostrada, American highway, Australian freeway or UK motorway, and anywhere else in the world with good-quality, high-speed roads or major twisty bits. Keep in mind water-cooled sports cars cope with sitting in heavy city traffic much better than air-cooled ones.

At the time of writing, the youngest available 1st generation 987 Boxster or Cayman is two years old and the oldest six: both types are excellent daily drivers, but are essentially useless for car-pooling. Keep in mind also that daily driving adds the miles and engine operating time, and will reduce (depreciate) the car's resale value more quickly than if it were a weekend warrior.

Why do you want one of these? (Courtesy Glen Marks)

A 987 Boxster or Cayman is an experience to be enjoyed, but does either type genuinely fit into your current lifestyle? Do you have a family? The models available in the 987 series are big boys' or girls' toys. The Porsche 987 Boxster and Cayman are often referred to as mid-life crisis fun machines designed for two consenting adults to enjoy in the fast lane. Being two-seaters, neither was ever meant to be anything but what they are, sports cars just for fun.

The ladies enjoy driving a Porsche sports car as much as the men ...
(Courtesy Porsche AG archive)

Are you prepared to look after a Boxster or Cayman? As with any thoroughbred it needs tender loving care, and it's not the type of car that can be started, and seconds later driven off, then parked after a short drive before the whole process is repeated. Sufficient time has to be given to get the oil, transmission fluid and coolant to start flowing properly. There are many electronic systems that need time to run through self-test routines before it's driven off.

What about exhaust noise? Is it going to impact your family or your neighbours, or attract the attention of local law enforcement? Standard 987 Boxster or Cayman models are quieter than earlier Porsche model series, but have still got a very distinct and noticeable sound about them and are louder than the average people carrier.

What about the money? You can afford to purchase a 987 Boxster or Cayman, but can you afford to own one? Are you prepared to pay the cost of ensuring your choice is always in peak roadworthy safe condition?

... the 987 series really provides a true sports car range for couples.
(Courtesy Porsche AG archive)

Are you prepared to purchase original parts? Are you prepared to pay a little more (not always the case with all tyre brands) to fit Porsche approved N-rated tyres?

The purchase of any 987 Boxster or Cayman model will impact your lifestyle, family and wallet; however the Porsche experience of a 987 model is worth every penny. The 987 Boxster and Cayman turns many heads amongst the general public. Both have shaken off the hairdresser's car image, James May (Captain Slow) of television's *Top Gear* fame owns a Boxster, and Hugh Laurie (TV's Dr House) owns a Cayman, and that's got to mean something, hasn't it?

4 Relative values
– which model for you?

The first questions that must be asked are either prefixed with: "What choices are there?" Or "What do I want?" When it comes to the Porsche 987 model range the choices might appear limited but, once options are taken into account, they are not. However, when it comes to major price drivers the overwhelming one is mileage. Research showed that the price differential (%) for similar specification cars of the same model year, one with low mileage (<20k) and the other with high mileage (>100k) was 60%. As a result calculating relative values between models is very complex as any accurate comparison must include variables such as national variant, exterior and interior colour combination, interior materials, solid or metallic paint, wheel, brake and transmission options, aftermarket modifications, condition, engine hours and mileage as mentioned above.

To avoid confusion relative values have been separated into the two main model ranges contained in the Porsche 987 series, starting with the Boxster model range.

987 Boxster

Approximate 987 Boxster model relative values are calculated using a datum point of 100% given to the most commonly available version which is the model year 2006 2.7-litre Porsche 987 Boxster with manual transmission.

Model year 2005 2.7-litre Boxster with manual transmission	90%
Model year 2005 2.7-litre Boxster with Tiptronic transmission	95%
Model year 2005 3.2 Boxster S with manual transmission	100%
Model year 2005 3.2 Boxster S with Tiptronic transmission	100%
Model year 2006 2.7-litre Boxster with manual transmission	100%
Model year 2006 2.7-litre Boxster with Tiptronic transmission	105%
Model year 2006 3.2 Boxster S with manual transmission	105%
Model year 2006 3.2 Boxster S with Tiptronic transmission	110%
Model year 2007 2.7-litre Boxster with manual transmission	100%
Model year 2007 2.7-litre Boxster with Tiptronic transmission	105%
Model year 2007 3.4 Boxster S with manual transmission	115%
Model year 2007 3.4 Boxster S with Tiptronic transmission	120%
Model year 2008 2.7-litre Boxster with manual transmission	105%
Model year 2008 2.7-litre Boxster with Tiptronic transmission	110%
Model year 2008 3.4 Boxster S with manual transmission	125%
Model year 2008 3.4 Boxster S with Tiptronic transmission	130%
Model year 2009 2.7-litre Boxster with manual transmission	115%
Model year 2009 2.7-litre Boxster with Tiptronic transmission	120%
Model year 2009 3.4 Boxster S with manual transmission	135%
Model year 2009 3.4 Boxster S with Tiptronic transmission	140%

Special Editions in the 1st generation 987 Boxster model range such as the 2.7-litre Sport Edition commands a minimum 25%, while the 3.2-litre Boxster S RS60 Spyder commands a minimum 50% premium over the preceding relative values.

987 Cayman

Approximate 987 Cayman model relative values are calculated using a datum point of 100% given to the most commonly available version which is the model year 2006 3.4-litre Porsche 987 Cayman S with manual transmission.

Model year 2005 2.7-litre Cayman with manual transmission	90%
Model year 2005 2.7-litre Cayman with Tiptronic transmission	95%
Model year 2005 3.4 Cayman S with manual transmission	100%
Model year 2005 3.4 Cayman S with Tiptronic transmission	105%
Model year 2006 2.7-litre Cayman with manual transmission	90%
Model year 2006 2.7-litre Cayman with Tiptronic transmission	95%
Model year 2006 3.4 Cayman S with manual transmission	100%
Model year 2006 3.4 Cayman S with Tiptronic transmission	105%
Model year 2007 2.7-litre Cayman with manual transmission	100%
Model year 2007 2.7-litre Cayman with Tiptronic transmission	105%
Model year 2007 3.4 Cayman S with manual transmission	115%
Model year 2007 3.4 Cayman S with Tiptronic transmission	120%
Model year 2008 2.7-litre Cayman with manual transmission	100%
Model year 2008 2.7-litre Cayman with Tiptronic transmission	105%
Model year 2008 3.4 Cayman S with manual transmission	130%
Model year 2008 3.4 Cayman S with Tiptronic transmission	135%
Model year 2009 2.7-litre Cayman with manual transmission	105%
Model year 2009 2.7-litre Cayman with Tiptronic transmission	110%
Model year 2009 3.4 Cayman S with manual transmission	135%
Model year 2009 3.4 Cayman S with Tiptronic transmission	140%

Special Editions in the 1st generation 987 Cayman model range such as the Cayman S Porsche Design Edition I and Cayman S Sport Edition command a minimum premium of 50% over the preceding relative values.

Note: In model year 2007 the 987 Boxster S was fitted with the same 3.4-litre engine used in the Cayman S. This accounts for the rise in relative value over its 3.2-litre powered older sister.

987 2.7-litre Boxster and 3.2-litre Boxster S models.
(Courtesy Porsche AG archive)

987 2.7-litre Cayman.
(Courtesy Porsche AG archive)

987 3.4-litre Cayman S.
(Courtesy Porsche AG archive)

987 Boxster S Orange (only 500 sold in
USA). (Courtesy Porsche AG archive)

3.4-litre 987 Boxster S RS60 Spyder.
(Courtesy Porsche AG archive)

3.4-litre 987 Cayman S with Sports Chrono
option package. (Courtesy Glen Marks)

3.4-litre 987 Boxster S Porsche Design
Edition II. (Courtesy Porsche AG archive)

3.4-litre 987 Boxster S Sport Edition with
PCCB. (Courtesy Porsche AG archive)

3.4-litre 987 Cayman S Porsche Design
Edition 1. (Courtesy Porsche AG archive)

5 Before you view
– be well informed

The key to a successful purchase is research! To avoid a wasted journey it will help if you're very clear about what questions you want to ask before you pick up the telephone. Some of these points might appear basic, but when you're excited about the prospect of buying your dream car it's amazing how some of the most obvious things slip the mind.

Check the current values of the model in which you are interested in car magazines, which provide price guides, and even auction results.

Where is the car?
Is it going to be worth travelling to the next county, state or to another country? A locally advertised car, although it may not sound very interesting, can add to your knowledge for very little effort, so make a visit – it might even be in better condition than expected.

Dealer or private sale?
Establish early on if the car is being sold by its owner or by a trader. A private owner should have all the history, so don't be afraid to ask detailed questions. A dealer may have more limited knowledge of a car's history, but should have some documentation. A dealer may offer a warranty/guarantee (ask for a printed copy) and finance. Private sales = no warranty and all legal liability on the purchaser's shoulders. Cost of collection and delivery? A dealer will be used to quoting for delivery using car transporters. A private owner may agree to meet you halfway, but only after you have seen the car at the vendor's address to validate the documents. Conversely, you could meet halfway and agree the sale but insist on meeting at the vendor's address for the handover.

View – when and where?
It is always preferable to view at the vendors home or business premises. In the case of a private sale, the car's documentation must tally with the vendor's name and address. Arrange to view only in daylight and avoid wet days (most cars look better in poor light or when wet).

Reason for sale?
Do make it one of the first questions. Why is the car being sold and how long has it been with the current owner? How many previous owners? Left-hand drive and right-hand drive models are available as Porsche manufactured its model range to comply with individual national requirements. There are nations with right-hand drive regulations that allow local registration of left-hand drive cars, but if left-hand drive is not permitted and private right-hand drive imports are restricted or banned, then a third party conversion may be your only choice, but explore all other avenues first.

Condition (body/chassis/interior/mechanicals)
Ask for an honest appraisal of the car's condition. Ask specifically about some of the check items described in chapter 7. A full systems check and test drive is

mandatory. A completely original 987 Boxster or Cayman's value is invariably higher than one with aftermarket modifications except the professionally tuned versions (think of the standard market price for the model and start by doubling it to get into the basic ball park).

Matching data/legal ownership/documentation

It's mandatory for any potential purchaser to ensure the VIN, engine number and license plate (if applicable) matches the official registration documentation. Is the owner's name and address recorded in the official registration documents? For those countries that require roadworthiness inspections such as an MoT certificate in the UK, or Fahrzeugausweis in Germany (TÜV) and Switzerland (MFK), does the car have a document showing it complies? If an exhaust and/or noise emissions certificate is mandatory, does the car have one? Does the car carry a current road tax or equivalent type sticker, or tag, as required in numerous countries such as the UK and Germany? Does the vendor own the car outright? Money might be owed to a finance company or bank: the car could even be stolen. Many nations have Government or private organisations that will supply for a fee accurate and complete vehicle ownership data, based on the car's licence plate number and/or VIN. These organisations can often also provide information related to the car's accident history such as: has the car previously been declared 'written-off' by an insurance company after an accident. In the UK the following organisations can supply vehicle data:

HPI	0845 300 8905
AA	0800 316 3564
DVLA	0300 790 6802
RAC	0330 159 0364

Unleaded fuel
The entire 987 series model range was designed to run on unleaded fuel only.

Insurance
Check with your existing insurer before setting out, your current policy, or that of the vendor, may not cover you to drive the car if you do purchase it. Do not drive uninsured cars and, if in doubt, always ask.

How can you pay?
A cheque (check) will take several days to clear and the seller may prefer to sell to a cash buyer. However, a banker's draft (a cheque issued by a bank) is a good as cash, but safer, so contact your own bank and become familiar with the formalities that are necessary to obtain one.

Buying at auction?
If the intention is to buy at auction see chapter 10 for further advice.

Professional vehicle check (mechanical examination)
There are often marque/model specialists who will undertake professional examination of a vehicle on your behalf. Owners' clubs will be able to put you in touch with specialists and Porsche dealerships offer similar services.

6 Inspection equipment
– these items will really help

Before you rush out of the door, gather together a few items that will help as you complete a more thorough inspection.

This book
Reading glasses (if you need them for close work)
Magnet (not powerful, a fridge magnet is ideal)
Torch (flashlight)
Probe (a small screwdriver works very well)
Overalls
Mirror on a stick
Digital camera
A companion

This book is designed to be your guide at every step, so take it along and use the check boxes to help you assess each area of the car you're interested in. Don't be afraid to let the seller see you using it.

Take your reading glasses if you need them to read documents and make close up inspections. The author has to take his off for close-up work, so carry a glasses case if you have to do the same.

A magnet will help you check if the car is full of filler, or has fibreglass or carbon-fibre panels. Ask the seller's permission before using a magnet: some may prefer you to use a paint depth meter. If permission is granted use the magnet to sample bodywork areas all around the car, but be careful not to damage the paintwork.

A torch with fresh batteries will be useful for peering into the front spoiler to check radiator condition, but remember both the Boxster and Cayman models have many panels covering up entire areas including the engine which is nicely hidden away.

A small screwdriver can be used – with care – as a probe, particularly in the wheel arches and on the underside. However, at the time of writing the entire 987 series model range will still be covered by the Porsche long life guarantee against corrosion. If structural corrosion is discovered do not use a probe, just advise the seller of your findings and walk away.

Be prepared to get dirty. Take along a pair of overalls, if you have them.

Fixing a mirror at an angle on the end of a stick may seem odd, but you'll probably need it to check the condition of the underside of the car. It will also help you to peer into some of the important crevices. You can also use it, together with the torch, along the underside of the sills and on the floor and remember that a completely original 987 Boxster or Cayman model is panelled the entire length of its underside.

A digital camera is a mandatory piece of inspection equipment. If you don't' have a digital camera use your mobile phone. Take lots of pictures of all parts of the car whether they cause you concern or not. When you get home study them and if in doubt, seek an expert's opinion. Sometimes photographs viewed in the quiet of your own home will reveal things you missed in the heat of the moment.

Have a friend or knowledgeable enthusiast accompany you: a second opinion is always valuable and also provides a level of personal security.

7 Fifteen minute evaluation
– walk away or stay?

Exterior

Ensuring the 987 Boxster or Cayman is parked on level ground, start the exterior inspection by looking for obvious signs of body damage and accident repairs.

Walk around the car, carefully placing the magnet onto random areas of the bodywork. If it sticks move on; if it not, find out why.

Corrosion (rust) damage is easy to spot as the paint will be bubbled and/or cracked. Measure the body panel gaps, around the front and rear luggage compartment lids and the doors. If the gaps are even it usually means the body is straight. Major

Check the panel gaps for consistency. (Author collection)

inconsistencies in gaps indicate the car has been repaired after a major accident.

Look for obvious signs of repainting, such as different shades and overspray.

Porsche paintwork is of the highest quality. The best place to look for overspray is in hard-to-get-at places, such as forward of the doors or under the wheel wells. A poor repaint is an immediate reason to walk away. A good quality repaint should not deter you from purchasing, but allow renegotiation of the price – downward! Inspect for minor front or rear end collisions by checking bumper mouldings for cracks and splits in the plastic.

Check around the headlight, foglight and indicator assemblies for stone chip damage and cracked lenses. With torchlight check the condition of the front-mounted radiators through the front spoiler. The number of radiators installed is model dependent. As a general rule 2.7-litre Boxster and Cayman models have two radiators (left and right) while the 3.2-litre Boxster S (model years 2005 and

2006), 3.4-litre Boxster S (model years 2007, 2008 and 2009) and the 3.4-litre Cayman S have three – centre front plus left and right radiators. One issue related to Porsche AG's excellent aerodynamic design is that as it draws cooling air into the radiator core(s) it also acts as a powerful vacuum cleaner, sucking up anything it can from the road surface. Ensure the radiators have been cleared of all debris. Organic materials decay (rot) and can cause all kinds of corrosion issues as the car ages.

987 Boxster S split rear spoiler (wing) extended. (Courtesy Porsche AG archive)

987 Cayman's rear spoiler (wing) extended. (Courtesy Porsche AG archive)

Check the condition of the rear lights' lens assemblies.

Check all seals; doors, hatchback (Cayman only), around all glass and all related to the moveable roof system fitted to the Boxster model range.

Ensure the seller extends the rear spoiler (wing) fully open, and inspect for any evidence of damage, rubbing or corrosion. Once completed ask the seller to retract the rear spoiler to its fully down position whilst you watch to ensure everything runs smoothly.

Whilst inspecting the exterior inspect the brake discs (rotors), callipers and pads. Pad friction material thickness must be greater than 2mm (0.08in) and the discs (rotors) must not be damaged. Check for evidence of brake fluid leakage over any components in the wheel wells, including at the rear of each wheel.

Check condition of the suspension components in the wheel wells.

Ask the seller to operate the Boxster's powered roof so that you can properly inspect the fabric as it's very expensive to replace. Ask the seller about any known roof repairs. Ensure the roof stowage cover also opens and closes smoothly. Check sealing, water drains, and condition of the glass rear window (Boxster) as well as the condition and alignment of the frame with the roof open and closed. There is an optional hard top available for the Boxster model range. If the sale includes such a roof assembly inspect for colour match, condition, and that all fittings are in good condition.

When carrying out an exterior inspection always check the ground under the car for evidence of fluid leaks: oil, coolant, transmission oil, water and/or hydraulic fluid.

Interior

Inspect all interior fittings and assemblies, including a full inspection of each seat for condition, ensuring none of the main or trim materials are cracked, torn, faded or missing. A cracked dash is extremely expensive to repair. Lower the rear seat backs and check behind. Inspect the instruments for damage or fading. Ensure the internal lighting system works.

Check all electric seat functions. If one set of controls is not working, it's possible that those functions were never installed by the factory, but check the options list. If seat heating is installed check this as well. These items are often overlooked and are expensive to repair. Ask the seller if there have been any problems with the airbags. Some owners disconnect the passenger airbag so children can occupy it: if disabled, ensure it's correctly labelled as such. Check that all the combined interior light and switch assemblies operate correctly, and inspect the light assemblies, which vary in location and design between models.

Check for moisture in the carpets and, if possible, check the condition of the control units installed under both seats, which vary depending on option status.

Run the electric windows down and back up to see if there's any moisture trapped in the door. Empty the contents of each door pocket and check for moisture. A good tip is to wipe the inside of each pocket with a tissue (Kleenex) to see if it picks up anything. Empty the contents of the glovebox (if installed) and check for evidence of moisture, damage to switches and cables; does the light come on? Check if there's an owner's manual somewhere in the car.

Compartments and mechanicals

Open both the front and rear luggage compartment lids on the Boxster. For the Cayman model the front luggage compartment lid and the hatchback/tailgate need to be opened and inspected. Ensure the luggage compartment lid gas struts hold it up. Inspect for condition any visible seals which run around the body in the vicinity of the lids/hatchback; check for any evidence of moisture. All the compartments are fully panelled and inspecting the items beneath requires the co-operation of the seller. There are easy items to inspect in the front luggage compartment such as the battery. Remove the plastic battery cover in the centre rear of the compartment, and inspect the battery for condition and any evidence of acid spill and/or corrosion. Check the compartment's panelled areas for moisture damage and staining. If everything is clean, what lies beneath is probably in good condition.

987 Boxster front luggage compartment. (Courtesy Porsche AG archive)

987 Cayman S front luggage compartment. (Courtesy Glen Marks)

987 Boxster rear luggage compartment. (Courtesy Porsche AG archive)

987 Cayman S hatchback rear compartment. (Courtesy Glen Marks)

Top of 2.7-litre Boxster engine exposed for a mandatory inspection. (Courtesy Bob Schoenherr)

Access to the 987 Cayman S 3.4-litre engine requires an empty rear compartment. (Courtesy Glen Marks)

No standard 987 model is fitted with a spare wheel and tyre assembly or jacking tools (optional spare tyre kit available for Boxster). However, a basic tool kit and a can of tyre inflating sealant is provided.

Accessing the engine in all models requires the assistance of the seller. Check the specific owner's manual for the engine access procedures. It may be easier with such new cars to try to do the engine inspection from underneath if the seller is unfamiliar with the engine access procedures.

Is it genuine and legal?

Ask the seller for all documentation related to the car, including owner's manual, service record book, emission inspection reports, any import documentation, mandatory roadworthiness inspection certificates, and all repair receipts.

Check the service record book; is it the original or a replacement (duplicate)? A duplicate record book will have 'Duplicate' stamped on each page.

Note: With the 987 series Porsche ceased installing its famous identification label on the underside of the front luggage compartment lid. All this information is now found in the vehicle data bank attached to the inside of the 'Maintenance' booklet. If this data bank is lost it cannot be re-ordered. Only the VIN, compliance stickers and tyre pressure labels are still physically attached to the car. The VIN is located on the windscreen (windshield), on a plate in the battery compartment, and possibly on some of the compliance stickers placed around the car, depending on national requirements.

The VIN on the windscreen (windshield) must match the VIN found at the previously mentioned locations in the car. Check the owner's manual for full details under Vehicle Identification chapter. Note: 1st generation Porsche 987 Boxster and Boxster S models, along with Cayman and Cayman S models, were either manufactured in Stuttgart Germany by Porsche AG or in Uusikaupunki Finland by Valmet. This means the 11th digit of the VIN will be 'S' for 987 models manufactured in Germany and 'U' for those manufactured in Finland.

A proper authenticity check should also include physically inspecting the engine ID plate, looking for its type and date of manufacture code and ensuring that these numbers match the type and codes in the vehicle's data bank. All numbers must match and must also match the national registration and insurance documents for the specific car being inspected. Paint code information is only shown in the vehicle's data bank.

Questions to ask the seller

There are some things that only the most experienced 1st generation 987 series expert is going to find during a 15 minute inspection. For the first time buyer it's much better to go armed with the important questions:

* Was this 987 model originally built for the market (country) it's being sold in?
* Has this car been used on track days, including driver education events, or been used in any form of motor sport?
* Is the mileage genuine?
* Is the car a weekend warrior or was it used as a daily driver?
* Was it regularly driven in heavy traffic?
* Has the car been involved in any accidents?
* Has the engine and/or transmission been repaired or modified?
* Does the car have the standard suspension or the optional Porsche Active Suspension Management (PASM) system?
* Are there any known problems with any of the car's electrical or electronic systems?

Common sense has to prevail with the buyer needing to recognise if they are being told the truth or not. If you purchase a 1st generation 987 with problems it can be extremely frustrating to repair.

Restoration of a basket case

There are very few 987 models if any (the author has not seen any) basket cases around and those that are, are usually accident wrecks. It's not worth purchasing a wreck as restoration at this time is not an economic option unless the purchase price is very low and you are a masochist. Maybe in a few years!

This cutaway diagram shows how the 987 Cayman's engine is accessed. (Courtesy Porsche AG archive)

8 Key points
– where to look for problems

Paying particular attention to, and understanding, what you are looking at!

Get up-close and personal.
(Author collection)

The concept of a hatchback (tailgate)
on a Porsche will be new to many, but
check its operation anyway.
(Courtesy Porsche AG archive)

987 Cayman front foglights inspection,
again, up-close and personal.
(Courtesy Porsche AG archive)

Get up-close and personal with the rear
lens assemblies, as well.
(Courtesy Porsche AG archive)

Radiators can be partially viewed through
the front spoiler on the Boxster range ...
(Author collection)

... and on the Cayman range.
(Courtesy Glen Marks)

To access one of the VIN plates (arrowed) the battery cover in the front luggage compartment has to be removed ... (Author collection)

... matching VIN in the windscreen (windshield). (Courtesy Glen Marks)

Are the wheels of the approved type? Inspect what's behind the spokes, too. (Courtesy Glen Marks)

All the factory and Porsche Exclusive options seen in this interior image can only be confirmed by reviewing the vehicle's data bank. (Courtesy Glen Marks)

9 Serious evaluation
– 60 minutes for years of enjoyment

Circle boxes for each check and add up points at the end of the inspection.
Excellent = 4, Good = 3, Average = 2 or Poor = 1

Any evaluation check must be realistic. Sole responsibility lies with the buyer to be vigilant and not cut corners over the next 60 minutes. Take the inspection seriously, get it right and you will be able to make an informed decision on whether to purchase, or not – and you keep your family relationships intact! Get it wrong and it could be your worst nightmare come true ...

First impressions count.
(Courtesy Glen Marks)

How does it look just sitting there?   4 3 2 1
Any model in the 987 series range is a thoroughbred sports car manufactured for high performance motoring. It is not a toy, and if it's not set up properly it will bite its owner. Before starting any evaluation ensure the Boxster or Cayman being inspected is parked on level ground. Does it sit level? Look at it from all angles. Is it clean inside and out? Does it look smart or a little tired? Does it smell of fast food? Does it look original? What's your first impression? The first rating is based on first impressions.

Exterior and interior colour combination   4 3 2 1
Everybody thinks at some time about the resale value of their cars. One huge value killer can be the exterior and interior colour combination. Men can be very practical on this subject and say: "I could get used to it" or "I can learn to live with it." Rating is for the honest opinions from all involved.

What about the exterior and interior colour combination? Does it work? (Courtesy Porsche AG archive)

Exterior paint   4 3 2 1
When inspecting a car's paintwork/bodywork

Seriously, you need to get up-close and personal when inspecting the paint. (Courtesy Porsche AG archive)

remember that it is always easier to repair/replace mechanical items than to do work of any type on the car's bodywork. A 987 Boxster or Cayman will be difficult to repair properly, especially structurally, and the Porsche workshop manual repair schemes are complicated, requiring specialist equipment. In reality there are two types of repairs that are carried out: (1) repair immediately at minimum cost and pass the problem to a new

Inspect the side air vents for condition, and to ensure they're not blocked. Plus, this is an easy way to distinguish between the 986 Boxster and a 987 Boxster, as the 987's side air vent is larger and more aerodynamic than that of its predecessor. (Courtesy Porsche AG archive)

owner; (2) keep the car after a thorough, high-quality repair (such permanent repairs are possible, but only if carried out by an experienced, professional who won't cut corners). This is why an inspection and assessment of the paintwork is so critical: how it's done is covered in chapter 7. If there are any doubts take as much time as you like before making an assessment decision. Rust is not an issue yet in the 987 series, but poor accident damage repairs have been identified within the Boxster community and rust could develop in the repaired areas. Rating is for condition.

Body panel general condition (including door bases)

Battle damage from debris on the road is a fact of life. A normal unmodified 987 sits significantly lower than standard road cars, and cars fitted with the optional PASM are even lower and always in the debris firing line. If there's no evidence of damage (stone chips, etc) on the front of the 987, check the mileage. A low-mileage car with no damage to the front is not unusual. However, high mileage but no frontal damage possibly indicates body panel repair and/or repainting. If in doubt ask the seller.

Body panel damage

Small dents and scrapes have to be assessed during the inspection. Scratches around the door locks and handles are quite normal, but the question for the buyer is always: Can the visible damage be repaired using the latest minor dent removal technologies, or is more serious and costly repair required?

Panel gaps

Walk around the car with a ruler and measure the gaps between all opening panels and surrounding metal work, which should all be even. Don't forget to compare one side of the car with the other. Rating is for irregularities in gap measurements and visible damage no matter how small or seemingly insignificant.

Cutaway diagram helps with locating components. (Courtesy Porsche AG archive)

Probably a good idea to remove the stuff in the front before inspection. Notice also that there's no spare wheel and tyre assembly installed. (Courtesy Porsche AG archive)

Brake fluid reservoir is located under this hatch in the front luggage compartment. (Courtesy Porsche AG archive)

Radiators are well protected behind the front spoiler, and access is difficult. (Courtesy Glen Marks)

Cutaway view of the Boxster's right side coolant radiator assembly. (Courtesy Porsche AG archive)

Seals

Boxster: Check the condition of all visible rubber seals, especially those around the front windscreen (windshield) and glass rear window of the rag top, around the door frames, and the front and rear luggage compartment. Don't forget to inspect all hardtop seals if it is included in the purchase.

Cayman: Check windscreen (windshield), hatchback, door frames, and the front luggage compartment.

Seal damage provides an entry path for water, which will cause problems later in the car's life. Rating is for condition and replacement cost if any seals are damaged.

Radiators & coolant colour

Radiator condition can only be assessed by a visual inspection of what can be seen through the front spoiler using a torch. If the Boxster or Cayman is fitted with air-conditioning, the condenser-mixer assemblies are actually mounted in front of the left and right side radiators

Check all 987 models' coolant colour by removing the blue cap. (Courtesy Glen Marks)

so it's the condenser-mixers that are really being inspected. The general rule is that if the mixers are in good condition the actual coolant radiators behind them should also be in good condition. If you want full access to the radiators for a detailed inspection, the front section underside panel and bumper moulding have to be removed. The number of coolant radiators installed varies: see chapter 7.

It's not possible to visually inspect all the individual components in the engine coolant system; however, a check of the coolant colour in the overflow/filling container in the rear luggage compartment of the Boxster, and inside the rear section of the interior of the Cayman, provides an excellent overview of system condition. Original coolant colour will be dependent on products used, but if the coolant has mixed with any other fluid in the engine, transmission or via one of the heat exchangers it will be muddy brown. If the current owner has not used the proper coolant/anti-freeze mixture, and used plain water instead it will also be muddy brown. Contaminated coolant is a reason to stop the inspection and walk away. Rating is for condenser-mixer/radiator assembly condition and coolant colour.

Lights ④ ③ ② ①
Check the condition and operation of all installed lighting systems front and rear, including headlights, rear lights, indicators (turn signals) front, rear and side, brake, reverse and foglights. Rating is for overall condition and correct operation.

Wipers ④ ③ ② ①
Boxster: Check condition and operation of the front wiper arm assemblies, including the wiper blades.

Cayman: Check condition and operation of front and rear window wiper arms and wiper blades. Rating is for condition and operation (don't forget to wet the glass first).

Washers ④ ③ ② ①
Check condition of the windscreen (windshield) and headlight (if installed) washer nozzles, and operate the system. Rating is for washer nozzle condition and spray operation.

Roadster rag top and hardtop ④ ③ ② ①
All 987 Boxsters are of the roadster body style, and were delivered as standard with an electric-powered rag top roof. A thorough inspection and functional check of the entire rag top system is highly recommended. All 987 Boxsters are fitted with a glass rear window. All roadster fabric roof systems creak, groan and moan, but the sound of fabric ripping can be very annoying as well as expensive to repair. Carry out an inspection with the roof fully up, in mid position, and fully down and stowed. Rating is for rag top fabric, frame, glass window and seal condition, and correct system operation.

An optional lightweight Porsche-manufactured hardtop was available for all Boxster models. If a hardtop is included in the purchase, ensure it's painted in the same colour as the Boxster's exterior. It should also be accompanied by specific Boxster installation accessories, so ensure these are present. Refer to the owner's manual for full details. Rating is for roof and accessories condition.

Correct operation of all lights must be ascertained.
(Courtesy Porsche AG archive)

Headlight washer nozzles, if installed, must also be inspected.
(Courtesy Porsche AG archive)

Ask the seller to operate the Boxster's roof.
(Courtesy Porsche AG archive)

What lies beneath? Every component in the Boxster's roof system must be inspected. (Courtesy Russ Standage)

Check the Roadster roof condition inside and out in various positions like this ... (Courtesy Ross Standage)

... and this ... (Courtesy Ross Standage)

... and this. (Courtesy Ross Standage)

Inspect the Boxster's heated rear window. (Courtesy Porsche AG archive)

Don't forget the hardtop if it's included with the Boxster. (Courtesy Porsche AG archive)

If viewing a Cayman the hatchback lid needs to be operated and inspected. (Courtesy Porsche AG archive)

Cayman hatchback (tailgate)

The 987 Cayman, Cayman S and Cayman special edition models are all fitted with a full length hatchback that can be opened and closed. Ensure the hatchback (tailgate) is opened to check all seals and related mechanisms; close and check fit for evenness. Rating is for condition and operation.

Windscreen (windshield)

Before carrying out a vehicle inspection find out what national rules apply to the windscreen (windshield) regarding acceptible damage. Is a single chip or crack sufficient to fail a mandatory roadworthiness inspection? Rating is for windscreen (windshield) condition and how it impacts roadworthiness.

Ensure the hatchback lid is fully supported by its gas struts, and that it stays up. (Courtesy Porsche AG archive)

Check the windscreen (windshield) for chips, cracks, and the VIN (arrowed). (Courtesy Glen Marks)

Door glass

⌊4⌋ ⌊3⌋ ⌊2⌋ ⌊1⌋

Operate the powered door windows. Ensure they move up and down freely without making any weird and wonderful sounds. Also check to see if any moisture is present on the glass after they have been run down and back up again. Check also that the windows seal correctly into the Boxster's rag top or Cayman's solid roof when both are fully up and locked. Rating is for condition, correct relative noiseless operation and detected moisture.

What rating should this wheel's condition receive? Is it approved for the 987 series? Yes! (Courtesy Porsche AG archive)

Inspect behind the wheel spokes. (Author collection)

Only a test drive is going to reveal wheel bearing issues. (Courtesy Porsche AG archive)

Wheels

⌊4⌋ ⌊3⌋ ⌊2⌋ ⌊1⌋

Check the wheels are correct for the model being inspected by comparing what's physically installed with the owner's manual. Incorrect wheels can cause serious problems, including wheel rub and unsafe handling. This inspection relates to safety as well as roadworthiness. If there's any doubt, ask the seller for additional paperwork on the wheels. The condition of each wheel is critically important as corrosion can lead to fatigue cracking and structural failure. Genuine Porsche factory wheels are clear coated, and if this coating is peeling it will be costly to get it repaired. Inspect for impact damage around the rim. Look at the relationship between the wheels and the wheelarch. Rating is for wheel originality and condition.

Wheel well linings

⌊4⌋ ⌊3⌋ ⌊2⌋ ⌊1⌋

Ensure all are fitted. Check condition of the plastic and mounting screws. Rating is for condition.

Wheel bearings and halfshafts

⌊4⌋ ⌊3⌋ ⌊2⌋ ⌊1⌋

Porsche wheel bearings are almost bullet proof and rarely fail. To check the wheel bearing, remove the wheel centre cap and, using a torch, inspect for evidence of metal filings and overheating. A failed wheel bearing will get very hot; will blue the cotter pin and burn the lubricating grease within the bearing, and wil deposit soot around the wheel bearing housing. If metal debris or evidence of overheating is discovered, jack the affected wheel off the ground and rotate it. If grinding or scraping noises are heard, it's likely either the wheel bearing and/or the halfshaft CV joint has failed. However, the test drive will reveal any rotating part with failed bearing surfaces because it will scream like a Banshee. Locating the source of the noise however, will require a thorough inspection. Rating is for condition of the wheel bearing and if a further more detailed inspection is warranted.

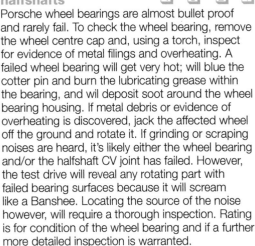

Tyre condition, suitability and wheel alignment

Who owns a thoroughbred sports car capable of high speeds and installs cheap tyres or mixes and matches tyre brands from side to side and front to rear in order to save money? Only a fool. The four black round bits of rubber wrapped around the wheels are the only things safely connecting the Boxster or Cayman to the road. Why spend huge amount of money purchasing a precision high performance sports car and then put everyone at risk by installing cheap useless tyres? A set of approved and tested tyres for the car not only gives it the ability to perform at its maximum in the handling department, but also allows the maximum transfer of power to the road and ensures the braking system provides maximum stopping power at all times.

See chapter 17 for Porsche approved tyres for the 987 series. (Courtesy Porsche AG archive)

The 987 Boxster and Cayman model range are designed to be driven on approved summer tyres in summer and the approved/tested winter tyres in winter: it was not designed around all-season el-cheapo jack-of-all trade tyres. Don't drive a Boxster or Cayman on summer tyres when the road temperature drops below 7°C (45°F), switch to winter tyres. Why? Winter tyres are made from a softer compound, heat up more quickly and don't go hard. To give just one example: if the road is wet and is at a temperature of 7°C (45°F) the summer tyres will require 38% more braking distance to stop from 80kph (50mph) to a full stop as compared to the winter tyres.

Unequal tyre wear is an indicator of wheel alignment issues. (Author collection)

Check tyres for same brand, same tread pattern, correct size front and rear for the installed wheels and in accordance with the owner's manual (see the table in chapter 17 which contains an up to date list of all tyres approved and tested by Porsche for the 987 series). Look at the wear across each tyre. Is it even? Is there more on the outside than inside, or vice versa? Bad wheel alignment will causes tyres to wear unevenly. Rating is for tyre condition (blisters and cracks), uneven wear, age (more than six years old), suitability and cost of a wheel alignment if required.

Steering system

All 987 Boxster and Cayman models are fitted with powered (boosted) rack and pinion steering. The power steering system requires the engine to be running, and any grinding and air cavitations noises from the engine mounted power steering pump will be obvious. With the engine running turn the steering wheel full left and then full right, listening for any unusual sounds.

Check under the middle and front of the car for any fluid leakage, which may not be immediately obvious, so slide some butcher's paper (described later under oil leaks) under the front and under right side of the engine, then come back later to check. Rating is for system component inspection and condition, static test with engine running and any detected fluid leaks.

Brake callipers and pads

The standard 2.7-litre 987 Boxster and Cayman models were fitted with black brake callipers. The 3.2-litre Boxster S, 3.4-litre Boxster S and 3.4-litre Cayman S models were fitted with red brake callipers. All models fitted with the optional PCCB system have yellow brake callipers. A basic brake calliper inspection can be carried out by

Standard 2.7-litre 987 Boxster is fitted with black 4-piston brake callipers. (Courtesy Porsche AG archive)

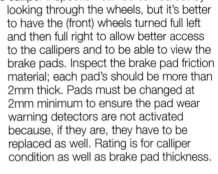

looking through the wheels, but it's better to have the (front) wheels turned full left and then full right to allow better access to the callipers and to be able to view the brake pads. Inspect the brake pad friction material; each pad's should be more than 2mm thick. Pads must be changed at 2mm minimum to ensure the pad wear warning detectors are not activated because, if they are, they have to be replaced as well. Rating is for calliper condition as well as brake pad thickness.

Standard 2.7-litre 987 Cayman also fitted with black 4-piston brake callipers. (Courtesy Porsche AG archive)

Brake discs (rotors)

All standard 987 models were delivered with steel perforated and ventilated front and rear brake discs (rotors). However, Porsche Ceramic Composite Brakes (PCCB) were offered on certain models.

Regardless of the type of brake disc (rotor) installed check each one, looking for cracks between the holes, blocked holes, grooves worn into the disc and other forms of wear. Consideration has to be given to overall brake disc (rotor) thickness which during such an evaluation is hard to check. Look at each disc carefully checking to see if there's a distinct lip or edge

PCCB, with its distinctive yellow brake callipers, is offered as an option on various 987 models. (Author collection)

4-piston red brake callipers are fitted to the 3.2- and 3.4-litre Boxster S models, and to the Cayman S model range. (Author collection)

around the outer circumference? Such a lip indicates that the brake pads have worn away both faces of the brake disc (rotor) and at the next service all discs will have to be replaced. Rating is for brake disc (rotor) condition and wear.

Hand (emergency/parking) brake

The hand brake (emergency/parking brake) must be tested to ensure it holds the car stationary under all circumstances. Rating is for brake holding ability.

987 Cayman S rear spoiler (wing) retracted. (Courtesy Porsche AG archive)

987 Boxster S rear spoiler (wing) extended. (Courtesy Porsche AG archive)

987 Cayman S rear spoiler (wing) extended. (Courtesy Porsche AG archive)

Rear spoiler (wing)

All models in the 987 range were delivered with a vertical moving electro-mechanical extend and retract rear spoiler (wing) system installed into the body directly behind the rear luggage compartment lid in the case of Boxster range and behind the hatchback (tailgate) in the Cayman model range. Ask the seller to extend it and, whilst the mechanism is running, ensure it does not bind or jam. Once it's fully extended check the condition of all visible parts. Ask the seller to retract it ensuring it retracts correctly, smoothly and it stows evenly. Rating is for rear spoiler (wing) condition and electro-mechanical operation.

Getting this engine compartment cover off the 987 Boxster is a drawn-out process. (Courtesy Bob Schoenherr)

Engine inspection

In every model in the 987 range the engine is the most difficult component to gain access to, as explained in chapter 7. In the Boxster the top of the engine (2.7, 3.2 or 3.4 litres) can only be accessed by carrying out a complicated exercise started by positioning the rag top roof in a specific position and then following all the procedures laid down in the owner's manual. The engine-driven belts, and some engine-driven accessories, can only be accessed by gaining access to and removing the engine bay panel located in the rear of the passenger

The front of the 987 Cayman's engine is accessed from a panel located behind the seats, just as in the 986 and 987 Boxster. (Courtesy Valerie Roedenbeck)

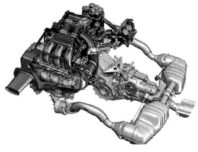

This is what you're looking to find under the covers. (Courtesy Porsche AG archive)

compartment. The underside of the engine can only be accessed from underneath. The Cayman 2.7 and 3.4-litre engines are accessed from inside the rear hatchback area, but there are no instructions in the owner's manual on how to do this. Ask the seller because you must gain access to the engine. When inspecting the engine ensure you are aware of what engine size should be installed. There are a few tuned 987s around, primarily by TechArt so it pays to know what you should find. Corrosion on the engine and associated components is quite common if the 987 has been driven in winter. Check for any visible forms of engine modifications. If anything causes alarm ask the seller relevant questions. Rating is for condition of all visible components, component originality, all visible metalwork and engine bay cleanliness.

Fuel cap cover and luggage compartments   4 3 2 1

The 987 series fuel cap cover is located on the right side wing (fender/guard) can be opened by hand anytime the Boxster or Cayman's doors are unlocked. Check the condition of the fuel cap and ensure the required labels installed on the cover's

Open the fuel cap and check for correct labelling.
(Courtesy Bob Schoenherr)

underside are correct and comply with national requirements. Check the fuel cap cover is locked when the car doors are locked.

The Boxster's luggage compartments lids and the Cayman's front luggage compartment and hatchback are released using electrical switches. Keep in mind that if the battery goes flat in either the Boxster or Cayman another battery is required to unlock the front luggage compartment lid to be able to access the flat battery fitted in the car. Starting with the front luggage compartment lid, lift it to its full open position and ensure the gas struts hold it open. Major fixed components in the front luggage compartment such as the fuel tank are not easily accessed. The battery cover can be removed and the battery and surrounds inspected. The tool kit is also accessible and can be easily inspected for condition. Sustained water ingress will cause the tools to rust. Move to the rear luggage compartment and ensure the gas struts hold it up as well. Inspect the carpet for condition and any evidence of water, coolant or oil. Coolant and oil systems are filled via access points in the rear luggage compartment.

987 Cayman S front luggage compartment.
(Courtesy Glen Marks)

987 Cayman front luggage compartment panels opened.
(Courtesy Glen Marks)

If a Cayman is being inspected open the rear hatchback (tailgate) and carry out the same inspection. The oil and coolant filler caps are under a cover in the rear of the compartment. Note: None of the 987 series model range is fitted with oil dipsticks. All fluid levels are monitored using electronic sensors.

Rating is for the condition of all components that can be reasonably inspected when the compartments are exposed, compartment condition and the presence and condition of all required accessories, tools and emergency equipment.

Battery charging rate

With the engine running at idle, connect a digital multi-meter across the battery terminals and the voltage shown on the display must be between 13.8 and 14.2 volts DC. To check battery condition, turn the off the engine and measure the voltage between the terminals again, it should be between 12.4 and 12.6 volts DC.

Rating is based on voltage measurements in both tests. For example: 13.8 volts DC and 12.6 volts DC = 4. More than 14.2 volts DC and less than 12.4 volts DC = 1.

Tow hook

The tow hook can be installed into a threaded section of the body structure, accessed through the front or rear bumper moulding (the holes are covered with a small, easily removed plastic cover). A quick check to ensure the unibody (combined chassis and body structure) is straight is to insert the tow hook. If the tow hook starts to resist and twists at an angle, or cannot even be inserted straight, this is a definite sign of an accident damaged and bent unibody. Rating is a pass with deductions for tow hook, bumper bar hole and cover condition. Walk away if the car fails this test.

Interior water ingress check

Open the doors and check along the bottom of each door for water. Run the electric door windows down and up to see if they pick up any moisture. Open each of the door storage compartments, checking for obvious signs of dampness or water damaged contents. Dab a Kleenex tissue around any suspect areas inside the car, including the carpets, to see if it picks up any moisture. Rating is for detected moisture.

Interior

The interior inspection is all about originality of installed seats, rollover bar, seatbelts, dashboard (instrument panel), carpet, mats and trim. Inspect for rips, tears, staining, mould, repairs and fraying seatbelts; is the seatbelt lower stitched loop still intact? (if it's been in an accident the loop will have been broken on impact), check the operation of seatbelt inertia reels front and rear, and for any other forms of damage. Check all the interior lights function when the doors are opened (on) and closed (off). Check all electrical and mechanical functions of the driver and passenger seats in accordance with the owner's manual. Check condition and operation of the wind deflector (Boxster only). Check condition of the rollover bar and its associated linings (Boxster

Interior: inspect for condition and originality.
(Courtesy Porsche AG archive)

Inspect and check operation of seat adjustment system.
(Courtesy Glen Marks)

Check condition of the Cayman's roof liner. (Courtesy Porsche AG archive)

Always inspect the seat backs for damage. (Courtesy Glen Marks)

only). Check the condition of the roof lining (Cayman only) Ensure the central locking and alarm systems function correctly. Rating is for condition, operation of electrical and mechanical seat functions, central locking, alarm system indication and interior lighting operation.

Instrument cluster close up. (Courtesy Porsche AG archive)

Instrument warning and advisory lights illuminated. (Courtesy Porsche AG archive)

Steering wheel, horn & steering column control stalks   4 3 2 1

Inspect the airbag steering wheel for condition. Check horn operation. Check all steering column stalk functions. Rating is for steering wheel condition, horn operation and condition and operation of each stalk lever.

Instruments   4 3 2 1

The 987 series was offered with numerous instrument dial and bezel colours in various materials including aluminium, carbon-fibre and wood. Check the car's option package, contained in the vehicle data bank, before concluding anything is not original. Check each instrument's internal lighting is functioning correctly when the headlights are turned on and check the light system dimming (the operation of which depends on installed options: check the owner's manual). Rating is for instrument condition and correct internal lighting operation.

Warning and advisory lights   4 3 2 1

Consult the owner's manual warning light system section as it's important to know what warning lights are fitted to a specific model and where everything is installed, including switches. Engage the hand (parking/emergency) brake and turn on the ignition, but do not start the engine. The warning system electronics will illuminate and then test all warning and advisory lights. Ensure all warning lights that should be are illuminated are. If there are any doubts read the owner's manual again or ask the seller. Rating is for condition of warning and advisory lights including symbols and correct operation.

The next stage is put the 987 onto a lifter or over a pit and carry out some basic inspections from underneath.

Lift the car and inspect underneath.
(Courtesy Russ Standage)

View from underneath with underside panels in place.
(Courtesy Russ Standage)

Oil filter exposed.
(Courtesy Bob Schoenherr)

Underside panels

All 987 models are fitted with a full set of underside panels: front, centre and rear. Check all are present and look closely for any evidence of scrape marks or impact damage. Never purchase a 987 Boxster or Cayman without its underside panels. Rating is for condition of panels.

Exhaust system

Much of the exhaust system can easily inspected from the underneath. Ask the seller if any exhaust modifications have been carried out. TechArt tailpipes are quite commonly installed. Rating is for exhaust system originality and condition.

Part of the 987 Cayman S exhaust system.
(Courtesy Glen Marks)

The entire exhaust system can be inspected from underneath.
(Courtesy Russ Standage)

Suspension

A visual inspection of the Boxster or Cayman wheel wells from underneath should reveal any suspension issues. Check for any aftermarket modifications to the suspension. If in doubt ask the seller. Rating is for suspension condition and detected aftermarket modifications.

It's better to inspect suspension components from underneath. (Courtesy Bob Schoenherr)

Oil leaks

One of the best oil leak checks that can be carried out is done after the test drive. Park the 987 on level ground and slide some butcher's paper under the engine, go away come back after thirty to sixty minutes. Pull out the paper and check how much oil has dripped on the paper. Rating is for any detected oil leaks during the static inspection and/or after the test drive.

Coolant leaks

Check the ground under the front spoiler, around each front wheel and underneath the rear of the car for any for any evidence of radiator coolant leakage. Rating is for detected leaks.

Transmission fluid and water leaks

Evidence of transmission fluid leaks and water leaks from the installed washer system can usually be detected in the vent holes of the underside panels. Rating is for detected leaks.

Test drive

This is mandatory. During the test drive every system must be tested including the air conditioning, heating, sound, etc. Everything with a button must be switched on and tested. The test drive rating must reflect the correct function of every system, handling, braking efficiency, acceleration and gear changing and the size of the smile on your face.

A test drive is mandatory; high-speed testing of brakes optional. (Courtesy Porsche AG archive)

With these modern cars there's no need to play hardball and create tension during the inspection. (Courtesy Russ Standage)

Playing hardball

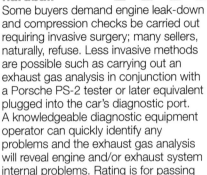

Some buyers demand engine leak-down and compression checks be carried out requiring invasive surgery; many sellers, naturally, refuse. Less invasive methods are possible such as carrying out an exhaust gas analysis in conjunction with a Porsche PS-2 tester or later equivalent plugged into the car's diagnostic port. A knowledgeable diagnostic equipment operator can quickly identify any problems and the exhaust gas analysis will reveal engine and/or exhaust system internal problems. Rating is for passing one or both tests, full points to null points (and walk away).

Evaluation procedure

Add up the points scored!

150 to 160 points = excellent to almost concours class, hope it doesn't break.
140 to 149 points = good to very good, but it's going to cost to keep it this way.
120 to 139 points = average to good, but where were the problems found?
110 to 119 points = below average to average and careful consideration required.
100 to 109 points = borderline money pit.
  80 to   99 points = beware it's going to cost a lot of money: what's the purchase price?
  79 points or less = run away, unless you want to turn a big fortune into a small one.

If any Porsche 987 Boxster or Cayman model scores less than 100 from such a detailed inspection the buyer needs to carefully consider their purchasing position because it's definitely going to be a money pit. Restoration of such a complicated piece of machinery to full roadworthiness is a labour of love as the money sunk into it cannot be recovered.

Rose-tinted glasses can cover a multitude of sins, but this puppy is a perfect example: top 1%. (Courtesy Glen Marks)

10 Auctions
– sold! Another way to buy your dream

Auction pros & cons
Pros: Prices will usually be lower than those of dealers or private sellers and you might grab a real bargain on the day. Auctioneers have usually established clear title with the seller. At the venue you can usually examine documentation relating to the vehicle.
Cons: You have to rely on a sketchy catalogue description of condition & history. The opportunity to inspect is limited and you cannot drive the car. Auction cars are often a little below par and may require some work. It's easy to overbid. There will usually be a buyer's premium to pay in addition to the auction hammer price.

Which auction?
Auctions by established auctioneers are advertised in car magazines and on the auction houses' websites. A catalogue, or a simple printed list of the lots for auctions might only be available a day or two ahead, though often lots are listed and pictured on auctioneers' websites much earlier. Contact the auction company to ask if previous auction selling prices are available as this is useful information (details of past sales are often available on websites).

Catalogue, entry fee and payment details
When you purchase the catalogue of the vehicles in the auction, it often acts as a ticket allowing two people to attend the viewing days and the auction. Catalogue details tend to be comparatively brief, but will include information such as "one owner from new, low mileage, full service history," etc. It will also usually show a guide price to give you some idea of what to expect to pay and will tell you what is charged as a 'Buyer's premium.' The catalogue will also contain details of acceptable forms of payment. At the fall of the hammer an immediate deposit is usually required, the balance payable within 24 hours. If the plan is to pay by cash there may be a cash limit. Some auctions will accept payment by debit card. Sometimes credit or charge cards are acceptable, but will often incur an extra charge. A bank draft or bank transfer will have to be arranged in advance with your own bank as well as with the auction house. No car will be released before all payments are cleared. If delays occur in payment transfers, then storage costs can accrue.

Buyer's premium
A buyer's premium will be added to the hammer price: don't forget this in your calculations. It is not usual for there to be a further state tax or local tax on the purchase price and/or on the buyer's premium.

Viewing
In some instances it's possible to view on the day, or days before, as well as in the hours prior to, the auction. There are auction officials available who are willing to help out by opening engine and luggage compartments and to allow you to inspect the interior. While the officials may start the engine for you, a test drive is out of the

question. Crawling under and around the car as much as you want is permitted, but you can't suggest that the car you are interested in be jacked up, or attempt to do the job yourself. You can also ask to see any documentation available.

Bidding

Before you take part in the auction, decide on your maximum bid – and stick to it!

It may take a while for the auctioneer to reach the lot you are interested in, so use that time to observe how other bidders behave. When it's the turn of your car, attract the auctioneer's attention and make an early bid. The auctioneer will then look to you for a reaction every time another bid is made; usually the bids will be in fixed increments until the bidding slows, when smaller increments will often be accepted before the hammer falls. If you want to withdraw from the bidding, make sure the auctioneer understands your intentions – a vigorous shake of the head when he or she looks to you for the next bid should do the trick! Assuming that you are the successful bidder, the auctioneer will note your card or paddle number, and from that moment on you will be responsible for the vehicle. If the car is unsold, either because it failed to reach the reserve or because there was little interest, it may be possible to negotiate with the owner, via the auctioneers, after the sale is over.

Successful bid

There are two more items to think about. How to get the Boxster or Cayman home and insurance? If you can't drive the car, your own or a hired trailer is one way; another is to have the vehicle shipped using the facilities of a local company. The auction house will also have details of companies specialising in the transfer of cars.

Insurance for immediate cover can usually be purchased on site, but it may be more cost-effective to make arrangements with your own insurance company in advance, and then call to confirm the full details.

eBay & other online auctions?

eBay & other online auctions could land you a high mileage 987 Boxster or Cayman at a bargain price, though you'd be foolhardy to bid without examining the car first, something most vendors encourage. A useful feature of eBay is that the geographical location of the car is shown, so you can narrow your choices to those within a realistic radius of home. Be prepared to be outbid in the last few moments of the auction. Remember, your bid is binding and that it will be very, very difficult to get restitution in the case of a crooked vendor fleecing you – caveat emptor!

Be aware that some cars offered for sale in online auctions are 'ghost' cars. Don't part with any cash without being sure that the vehicle does actually exist and is as described (usually pre-bidding inspection is possible).

Auctioneers

Barrett-Jackson
www.barrett-jackson.com
Bonhams www.bonhams.com
British Car Auctions (BCA)
www.bca-europe.com or
www.british-car-auctions.co.uk
Cheffins www.cheffins.co.uk

Christies www.christies.com
Coys www.coys.co.uk
eBay www.ebay.com
H&H www.classic-auctions.co.uk
RM www.rmauctions.com
Shannons www.shannons.com.au
Silver www.silverauctions.com

11 Paperwork
– correct documentation is essential!

Example of the Porsche vehicle data bank system supplied to owners of 1st generation 987 Boxsters and Caymans. (Courtesy Valerie Roedenbeck)

The paper trail
Porsche cars usually come with a large portfolio of paperwork accumulated and passed on by a succession of proud owners. This documentation represents the real history of the car and from it can be deduced the level of care the car has received, how much it's been used, which specialists have worked on it and the dates of routine maintenance, major repairs and restorations. All of this information will be priceless to you as the new owner, so be very wary of cars with little paperwork to support their claimed history.

Registration documents
All countries/states have some form of registration for private vehicles whether it's like the American 'pink slip' system, German TÜV, Swiss MFK or the British 'log book' systems.

It is essential to check that the registration document is genuine, that it relates to the car in question, and that all the vehicle's details are correctly recorded, including chassis/VIN and engine numbers (if these are shown). If you are buying from the previous owner, his or her name and address will be recorded in the document: this mayl not be the case if you are buying from a dealer. In the UK the current (Euro-aligned) registration document is named 'V5C,' and is printed in coloured sections of blue, green and pink. The blue section relates to the car specification, the green section has details of the new owner and the pink section is sent to the DVLA in the UK when the car is sold. A small section in yellow deals with selling the car within the motor trade. In the UK the DVLA will provide details of earlier keepers of the vehicle upon payment of a small fee, and much can be learned in this way. If the car has a foreign registration there may be expensive and time-consuming formalities to complete. Do you really want the hassle?

Roadworthiness certificate

Most country/state administrations require that vehicles are regularly tested to prove that they are safe to use on the public highway and do not produce excessive emissions. In the UK that mandatory test (the 'MoT') is carried out at approved testing stations, for a fee. In states of the USA the requirement varies, with some states only insisting on mandatory emissions tests at regular intervals. In nations such as Switzerland and Germany such roadworthiness tests are mandatory supported by random Police controlled inspections.

In the UK the test is required on an annual basis once a vehicle becomes three years old. Of particular relevance for older cars is that the certificate issued includes the mileage reading recorded at the test date and, therefore, becomes an independent record of that car's history. Ask the seller if previous certificates are available. Without an MoT the vehicle should be taken on a flat-bed to its new home, unless you insist that a valid MoT is part of the deal, which is best because it's another inspection by another set of eyes.

Road licence

The administration of every country/state charges some kind of tax for the use of its road system, the actual form of the 'road licence' and, how it is displayed, varying enormously country to country, and state to state. Whatever the form of the 'road licence', it must relate to the vehicle carrying it and must be present and valid if the car is to be driven on the public highway legally. The value of the license will depend on the length of time it will continue to be valid. In the UK if a car is untaxed because it has not been used for a period of time, the owner has to inform the licensing authorities, otherwise the vehicle's date-related registration number will be lost and there will be a painful amount of paperwork to get it re-registered. Changed legislation in the UK means that the seller of a car must surrender any existing road fund licence, and it is the responsibility of the new owner to re-tax the vehicle at the time of purchase and before the car can be driven on the road. It's therefore vital to see the Vehicle Registration Certificate (V5C) at the time of purchase, and to have access to the New Keeper Supplement (V5C/2), allowing the buyer to obtain road tax immediately.

Certificates of authenticity

For most Porsche models it is possible to obtain a certificate proving the age and authenticity (eg engine and chassis numbers, paint colour and trim). If you want to obtain one, the only place to start is with your local Porsche dealer, but there is a cost involved and in some countries it's not possible to obtain a Certificate of Authenticity.

If the car has been used in European classic car rallies it may have a FIVA (Federation Internationale des Vehicules Anciens) certificate. The so-called 'FIVA Passport', or 'FIVA Vehicle Identity Card,' enables organisers and participants to recognise whether or not a particular vehicle is suitable for individual events. If you want to obtain such a certificate go to www.fbhvc.co.uk or www.fiva.org there will be similar organisations in other countries too.

Valuation certificate
Hopefully, the vendor will have a recent valuation certificate, or letter signed by a recognised expert stating how much he, or she, believes the particular car to be worth (such documents, together with photos, are usually needed to get 'agreed value' insurance). Generally such documents should act only as confirmation of your own assessment of the car rather than a guarantee of value as the expert has probably not seen the car in the flesh. The easiest way to find out how to obtain a formal valuation is to contact the owners club.

Service history
Try to obtain as much service history and other paperwork pertaining to the car as you can. Naturally, dealer stamps, or specialist garage receipts score most points in the value stakes. However, anything helps in the great authenticity game: items like the original bill of sale, handbook, parts invoices and repair bills, adding to the story and the character of the car. Even a brochure correct to the year of the car's manufacture is a useful document and something that you could well have to search hard to locate in future years. If the seller claims that the car has been restored, then expect receipts and other evidence from a specialist restorer.

If the seller claims to have carried out regular servicing, ask what work was completed, when, and seek some evidence of it being carried out. Your assessment of the car's overall condition should tell you whether the seller's claims are genuine.

Restoration photographs
If the seller tells you that the car has been restored, then expect to be shown a series of photographs taken while the restoration was under way. Pictures taken at various stages, and from various angles, should help you gauge the thoroughness of the work. If you buy the car, ask if you can have all the photographs as they form an important part of the vehicle's history. It's surprising how many sellers are happy to part with their car and accept your cash, but want to hang on to their photographs! In the latter event, you may be able to persuade the vendor to get a set of copies made.

12 What's it worth?

– let your head rule your heart

Heart and head

I believe you will know the right Porsche for you. It's the one that puts a permanent smile on your face and causes your heart to race like the first time you were in love! But this is a cruel world and you must not let your heart rule your head because, if you get it wrong, your heart will sink and that may just be the start of your troubles ...

Condition

If the car you've been looking at is really bad, then you've probably not bothered to use the marking system in chapter 9 – 60 minute evaluation. You may not have even got as far as using that chapter at all!

If you did use the marking system in chapter 9 you'll know whether the car is in excellent (maybe concours), good, average or poor condition or, perhaps, somewhere in-between these categories. Many car magazines run a regular price guide. If you haven't bought the latest editions, do so now and compare their suggested values for the model you are thinking of buying: also look at the auction prices they're reporting. Values have been fairly stable for some time, but some models will always be more sought-after than others. Trends can change too. The values published in the magazines tend to vary from one magazine to another, as do their scales of condition, so read carefully the guidance notes they provide. Bear in mind that a car that is truly a recent show winner could be worth more than the highest scale published. Assuming that the car you have in mind is not in show/concours condition, relate the level of condition that you judge the car to be in with the appropriate guide price. How does the figure compare with the asking price? Before you start haggling with the seller, consider what affect any variation from standard specification might have on the car's value. If you are buying from a dealer, remember there will be a dealer's premium (profit margin) on the price as they have to feed their families as well.

Desirable options/extras
- Porsche design option package
- Sport model option package
- Chrono sport option packages

Undesirable features
- Repainted and/or the original colour changed
- Unapproved aftermarket wheels and tyres (incorrect size and offset)
- Noisy aftermarket exhaust modifications
- Non-Porsche aerodynamic additions

Warranty

Commercial car dealers have to provide a minimum period of warranty on certain items on any car, but in the real world is the warranty worth the paper it's written on? Look around; is this dealer capable of dealing with repairing sophisticated Porsche engineering? What's covered by the warranty? How far from the dealer do you live? How are you going to get the car back to the dealer? What about purchasing extended warranty policies? Ask yourself the same questions. Is the company underwriting the warranty policy going to be around in two years? Warranties, unless purchasing from a reputable approved Porsche dealer, should not be a purchase consideration as, in the real world, nine out of ten times when something fails it is not going to be repaired under any warranty scheme without a fight which more often than not the buyer loses. Maybe it might be worth getting a discount on the purchase price and foregoing the warranty altogether?

Private purchases are not protected by mandatory warranty requirements and getting a previous owner to pay for undisclosed problems and any repairs usually involves legal action.

Pre-purchase inspection (PPI)

This buyer's guide contains many procedures that you as the buyer can follow, but I still strongly recommend that any 1st generation 987 model being seriously considered for purchase be taken to a recognised expert, usually a Porsche dealer for a fully independent inspection. A PPI should also detect any legal issues such as forged registration papers which are becoming an ever increasing problem in the United Kingdom after the theft of hundreds of thousands of official V5 forms in 2006. Ringing of VINs or detecting clones of legally registered cars does require expertise, but nothing is ever guaranteed. You will have to pay for such an inspection, but it's worth it.

Striking a deal

Negotiate on the basis of your condition assessment, mileage and fault rectification cost. Also take into account the car's specification. Be realistic about the value, but don't be completely intractable: a small compromise on the part of the vendor or buyer will often facilitate a deal at little real cost. However, it's critical that you use your evaluation points score as your basis for negotiating the price down. If you have identified problems that from this guide or from other sources you know are going to cost a lot of money to rectify, you must insist these costs are deducted from the final purchase price. Just one failed electronic unit can cost a lot of money, so why pay for it if you already know it's failed? It's far better to walk away from a deal than to let your heart rule your head. There is always a better deal out there ... somewhere.

13 Do you really want to restore?
– it'll take longer and cost more than you think

A Porsche 987 Boxster or Cayman model is not a normal car. Its unibody or monocoque construction is an extremely complicated piece of design and engineering. It's very difficult to pull apart, repair and put back together properly. The biggest issue with structural repair is getting all the right parts, jigging and clamping them correctly into position, welding accurately and treating the metalwork, including the weld joints to ensure that rust cannot form in and around the repair during the restoration and after it's all been painted.

That's got to hurt and, sadly restoration is not possible ...
(Courtesy Porsche AG archive)

Specialist tools and equipment – including a proper assembly jig – is required for all structural repairs, as is the factory workshop structural repair manual, which must be followed to the letter. There are no short cuts when you want to properly repair a car's structure, and the likely need for new coolant radiators for crash-damaged cars adds to the overall complexity and cost. Standard and optional electrical, electronic and mechanical systems installed in the 987 model range are complicated, and components such as system control units extremely expensive to purchase. Damaged wiring looms are a nightmare to repair.

... ditto.
(Courtesy Porsche AG archive)

In summary, each of these cars is a piece of precision engineering that does not lend itself easily to major restoration, but if you're not convinced, read on, McDuff ...

Questions and answers
The biggest cost in any restoration is labour: can you do it all yourself or do you need professional help?

• How are your welding and painting skills?
• Do you have the required tooling and specialist equipment including a monocoque jig for any structural repairs?
• Do you have the Porsche workshop structural repair manual?
• Do you have the facilities?
• Do you have an approved Porsche dealer nearby?
• Do you have the time?
• How long do you expect it to take? Your dedication is high now, but what's it going to be in two years?

- If you cannot do the work yourself, can you afford professional restoration? A full external and internal restoration including engine and transmission rebuilds is going to cost a huge amount in any currency.
- Is a rolling chassis restoration an option? Good luck in finding one.
- In theory if a full 'nut & bolt' restoration is intended it's usually best to buy the worst car you can find, so long as certain components are good, but how will you know what's good and what's not without specialist test equipment and knowledge?
- Will the money ploughed into a full restoration ever be recovered? Not a chance! In the Porsche world originality is always worth more than restored.

A 987 Boxster or Cayman restoration can only be approached as a labour of love as it makes no economic sense. It's actually much cheaper to buy a fully functional higher mileage example. Note: At the time of writing a 1st generation 987 Cayman rolling chassis was advertised for sale on the internet in the United Kingdom, but no photographs were forthcoming.

This 987 Boxster might appear restorable, but it will be an expensive project, and not very cost-effective. (Author collection)

Serious crash damage and not a realistic restoration project ... (Author collection)

... ditto ... (Author collection)

... and again. (Author collection)

14 Paint problems
– bad complexion, including dimples, pimples and bubbles

Paint faults generally occur due lack of protection and/or maintenance, or to poor preparation prior to a repaint or touch-up. Some of the following conditions may be present in the car you're looking at:

Orange peel (bad)
Most Boxsters and Caymans left the factory with a slight orange peel look. However, bad orange peel an uneven paint surface, similar to the appearance of the skin of an orange. The fault is caused by the failure of atomized paint droplets to flow into each other when they hit the surface. It's sometimes possible to rub out the effect with proprietary paint cutting/rubbing compound or very fine grades of abrasive paper. A repaint may be necessary in severe cases. Consult a bodywork repairer/paint shop for advice on the particular car.

987 Boxster in the Porsche paint shop ... (Courtesy Porsche AG archive)

Cracking
Severe cases are likely to have been caused by too heavy an application of paint (or filler beneath the paint). Also, insufficient stirring of the paint before application can lead to the components being improperly mixed, and cracking can result. Incompatibility of new paint with the paint already on the panel can have a similar effect. To rectify the problem it is necessary to rub down to a smooth, sound finish before repainting the problem area. Rolling of wings (fenders/guards) can also cause cracking.

... ditto ... (Courtesy Porsche AG archive)

Crazing
Sometimes the paint takes on a crazed rather than a cracked appearance when the problems mentioned under 'Cracking' are present. This problem can also be caused by a reaction between the underlying surface and the paint. Paint removal and repainting the problem area is usually the only solution. Painted thermal plastics will craze over time.

... this process always resulted in a slight orange peel effect finish. (Courtesy Porsche AG archive)

Blistering
Very rare, but when it does occur it's always caused by rust developing underneath the paint. Usually perforation will be found in the metal and the damage will usually be worse than that suggested by the area of blistering. The metal will have to be repaired before repainting.

Micro blistering
Usually the result of a cheap repaint. Consult a paint specialist, but usually damaged paint will have to be removed before partial or full repaint.

Fading and oxidation
Some colours, especially solid reds, are prone to fading and oxidation if subjected to strong sunlight for long periods without constant polish protection. Sometimes proprietary paint restorers and/or paint cutting/rubbing compounds will retrieve the situation. Often a repaint is the only real solution.

Look after its paint and your Cayman S will remain in pristine condition for years.
(Author collection)

Peeling
Often a problem with metallic paintwork begins when the sealing lacquer becomes damaged and begins to peel off. Poorly applied paint may also peel. The remedy is to strip and start again!

Dimples
Caused by the residue of polish (particularly silicone types) not being removed properly before repainting. Paint removal and repainting is the only solution.

Dents
Small dents are usually easily fixed by the 'Dentmaster,' or equivalent process, that sucks or pushes out the dent (as long as the paint surface is still intact). Companies offering dent removal services usually come to your home: consult your telephone directory.

Even the most sophisticated Porsche paint schemes are known for their durability ...
(Courtesy Porsche AG archive)

... ditto.
(Courtesy Porsche AG archive)

15 Problems due to lack of use

– just like their owners, Porsche 897s need exercise!

Dolly Parton was asked once why she was still working as hard as ever in the music industry. She answered: "I'd rather wear out than rust out." Letting a 987 stand unused will ensure it develops some problems.

So, what can happen if a 987 is not used and just sits?

Internal corrosion

All 987 models are fitted with a wet-sump horizontally opposed six-cylinder engine meaning that, when it's switched off, most of the oil is retained inside the engine, albeit in what Porsche call an internal oil-tank. The only protection against the onset of corrosion once the engine is stationary is the oil film left on the engine's components and, if the engine remains stationary for a period of time, gravity takes over and the oil drains away and leaves areas of bare metal unprotected. Over a long period of lack of use corrosion will start on any

Non-use during winter storage can create minor problems, but it's much better than exposing the Cayman to salted roads. (Courtesy Porsche AG archive)

unprotected exposed areas of bare metal, but that's not all, there's another problem. Oil starts to break down (separates into various chemical compounds). Depending on the type of oil used some of the chemical compounds may recombine forming an acidic residue which corrodes any exposed metal it comes in contact with. Modern petrol blends with ethanol content greater than 10% will also cause internal corrosion of the fuel delivery system right up to the fuel injectors. Corroded metal fuel manifold lines will result in fuel leaks and present a real danger of fire when the engine starts.

Seized components

Pistons in brake callipers will seize caused by corrosion as the dust caps and seals dry out, crack and fail.

Moisture in the brake fluid which is used in many systems will start internal system corrosion. The main components affected are: the brake master cylinder, clutch slave cylinder and ABS hydraulic unit. If the internals have corroded it's quite possible that horrendous problems will occur when the Boxster or Cayman is started.

Steel brake discs (rotors) rust and the brake pads may also stick to them.

The clutch may seize if the plate becomes stuck to the flywheel because of corrosion. Handbrakes (emergency/parking brakes) will seize as cables and linkages rust. In the 987 series the handbrake assembly is installed in the rear wheel hubs: old technology, quite complicated and, yes, expensive to repair.

Internal seals
Without fluid for lubrication even synthetic rubber seals will start to dry out and break down. The 987 engine series all use large numbers of o-rings and gaskets and long-term storage without due care and attention will result in many oil leaks once it's started again. The same issue applies in the braking system.

External seals
As time passes all the rubber sealing used to protect the car against water ingress will harden, crack, and fail.

Fluids
Old acidic engine oil will corrode any exposed metal it can get to. Brake fluid absorbs water from the atmosphere and must be renewed every two years.

Untreated water left in the windscreen (windshield) washer system will stagnate.

Tyres and wheels
Tyres that have had the weight of the car on them in one position for some time will develop flat spots, resulting in driving vibration. The tyre walls may develop cracks or (blister-type) bulges, and aged rubber (over 6 years) can become too hard and unsafe.

Corroded wheels are expensive to repair and/or replace.

MacPherson struts and shock absorbers (dampers)
Without use damper seals will fail, allowing the gas used as part of the internal damping system to escape, and collapse often. If the 987 is fitted with the optional and much more complicated Porsche Active Suspension Management (PASM) system components, any damage caused by lack of use will be much more expensive to repair.

Recharging a flat battery is a common lack of use issue. (Author collection)

Rubber and plastic
Rubber is used throughout the car in various mounts for the transmission and suspension, and in bushings. once it goes hard and cracks all sorts of grunts, groans, vibrations and, in the worst case scenario, handling problems can occur.

Fuel hoses are made from rubber, as are many of the engine oil system interconnects. Once these hoses perish there is a serious risk of fire.

Halfshaft (driveshaft) CV joints and steering arms have rubber covers (boots) and when they crack it allows the outside environment into sensitive lubricated components which will eventually fail.

Electrics
Leaving a battery installed and not driving the car can result it going completely flat in less than four weeks and in winter it will die faster. A lead acid battery left discharged for long periods of time will not be capable of being recharged and will have to be replaced.

Exhaust system
Exhaust gas always contains water. Water sitting for long periods of time in a cold exhaust system will cause it to rot from the inside. The outside of the exhaust system will also rust caused by corrosive elements in the atmosphere or from salt and other road grime stuck to it.

Mould
Most of the 987 model range is fitted with full leather interiors. Any moisture inside the car with the right environmental conditions will result in mould growing in the leather and spreading throughout the entire interior.

Mould will ruin leather. Take care to protect the interior against mould when the car is in storage, even if it's only for a short time, and especially in moist environments. (Author collection)

16 The Community
– key people, organisations and companies in the 987 world

This chapter provides various sources that prospective 987 Boxster or Cayman owners can seek advice and guidance from, what's available to read, and which organisations to join if a purchase is made.

Books
Porsche Cayman: Thrill of the Chase, by Jutta Deiss, published by Motorbooks International, ISBN: 0760325812 and 978-0760325810.

Porsche: Excellence Was Expected. The Comprehensive History of the Company, its Cars and its Racing Heritage 2008 Edition, by Karl Ludvigsen, published by Bentley Publishing, ISBN: 978-0-8376-0235-6.

Magazines
There are no specific 987 Boxster or Cayman magazines. However, in many Porsche club magazines both the Boxster and Cayman and their owners frequently appear in print, and may have dedicated sections/experts.

Porsche major assembly rebuild and/or exchange services
Note that regional and national clubs will also be able to provide details of specialists in your part of the world.

Autofarm (1973) Ltd
Oddington Grange
Weston-on-the-Green
Oxfordshire
OX25 3QW
England
Tel: +44 (0)1865 331234
www.autofarm.co.uk

Sportec AG
Hofstrasse 17
CH-8181 Höri bei Bülach/ZH
Switzerland
Tel: +41 (0) 43 411 43 00
www.sportec.ch

Porsche parts suppliers
Porsche Centre Hatfield
1 Hatfield Avenue
Hatfield Business Park
Hatfield
Hertfordshire
AL10 9UA

England.
Tel: +44 (0) 1707 277911
www.porschehost.com/home.asp?opc=hatfield

Porsch-Apart Ltd
Unit 4 Field Mill
Harrison Street
Ramsbottom
Bury
Lancashire
BL0 0AH
England
Tel: +44 (0) 1706 824053
www.porsch-apart.co.uk

Porsche clubs
The author has been involved with some UK and European based Porsche clubs in the past and is happy to recommend:

Porsche Club Great Britain Registered Office
Cornbury House
Cotswold Business Village, London Road
Moreton-in-Marsh
Gloucestershire
GL56 0JQ
England
Tel: +44 (0)1608 652911
http://www.porscheclubgb.com

TIPEC Club Office (The Independent Porsche Enthusiasts Club)
10 Whitecroft Gardens
Woodford Halse
Northants
NN11 3PY
England
Tel: +44 (0) 8456 020052
http://www.tipec.net

Internet-based Porsche communities
For North American readers please check with the Porsche Club America website (www.pca.org) to find the contact address of the PCA regional group nearest to you.

Google is your friend. Use the search words 'Porsche 987' or 'Boxster' or 'Cayman' to get started, or check these out:

http://www.caymanclub.net/
http://www.planet-9.com/

Production numbers

1st generation 987 Boxster and Cayman production figures		
Model year	**Model**	**Number manufactured**
2005	Boxster	10,289
	Boxster S	9189
	Cayman	29
	Cayman S	145
2006	Boxster	8861
	Boxster S	5522
	Cayman	2058
	Cayman S	14,239
2007	Boxster	6761
	Boxster S	4856
	Boxster Orange	56
	Boxster S Orange	54
	Cayman	7680
	Cayman S	7305
2008	Boxster	4895
	Boxster S	2786
	Boxster Orange	195
	Boxster S Orange	197
	Boxster S RS60	1958
	Boxster Sport	300
	Boxster S Sport	200
	Boxster S Porsche Design Edition 2	3
	Cayman	5583
	Cayman S	5351
	Cayman S Porsche Design Edition 1	777
	Cayman S Sport	3
2009	Boxster	572
	Boxster S	231
	Boxster S RS60	6
	Boxster S Porsche Design Edition 2	383
	Cayman	665
	Cayman S	196
	Cayman S Sport	629

Type M96 engine specifications*

Engine type	M96.25	M96.26
Bore mm (in)	85.5 (3.37)	93 (3.66)
Stroke mm (in)	78 (3.07)	

Displacement cc (in³)	2687 (163.96)	3179 (193.98)
Compression ratio	11.0:1	11.0:1
Horsepower (Kw/hp)@rpm	176/240@6400	206/280@6200
Torque (Nm/ft-lb)@rpm	270/199@4700-6000	320/236@4700-6000
Maximum rpm	7200	
Fuel octane	95 to 98 RON (90 to 93 CLC or AKI) premium unleaded	
Fuel consumption L/100km (mpg)	8-11L 100km (21-27mpg)	
Oil press@5000 rpm (oil temp 90°C/194°F)	6.5 bar (94psi)	
Oil consumption	1.5-litre per 1000km (1.59 US quarts per 621 miles)	

Used in the 987 Boxster and Boxster S model range for model years 2005 and 2006 only.

Type M97 engine specifications*

Engine type	M97.20	M97.21	M97.22
Bore mm (in)	85.5 (3.37)	96 (3.78)	
Stroke mm (in)	78 (3.07)		
Displacement cc (in³)	2687 (163.96)	3387 (206.67)	
Compression ratio	11.0:1		
Horsepower (Kw/hp)@rpm	180/245@6500	217/295@6250	223/303@6250
Torque (Nm/ft-lb)@rpm	273/201@4600-6000	340/251@4400-6000	
Maximum rpm	7200	7300	
Fuel octane	95 to 98 RON (90 to 93 CLC or AKI) premium unleaded		
Fuel consumption L/100km (mpg)	8-11L 100km (21-27mpg)		
Oil press@5000 rpm (oil temp. 90°C/194°F)	6.5 bar (94psi)		
Oil consumption	1.5-litre per 1000km (1.59 US quarts per 621 miles)		

Used in the Boxster, Boxster S, Cayman and Cayman S model range for model years 2007 to 2009.

Transmission types*

Designation	Model year(s)	Type and model application
G87.01	2005 to 2009	5-speed manual for 2.7L** Boxster and Cayman
A87.01	2005 to 2006	5-speed Tiptronic S for 2.7L Boxster
G87.20	2005 to 2006	6-speed manual for 3.2-litre Boxster S
A87.20	2005 to 2006	5-speed Tiptronic S for 3.2L Boxster S
G87.20***	2007 to 2009	6-speed manual for 2.7L Boxster and Cayman
A87.02	2007 to 2009	5-speed Tiptronic S for 2.7L Boxster and Cayman
	2005 to 2009	
G87.21	2007 to 2009	6-speed manual for 3.4-litre Boxster S and Cayman S
	2005 to 2009	
A87.21	2007 to 2009	5-speed Tiptronic S for 3.4-litre Boxster S and Cayman S
	2005 to 2009	

Limited slip differential (LSD) was not offered as an option on any 987 series transmissions.

**L = litres*

***Option I480*

987 series brake system specifications

987 Model	Boost system	Front callipers / Rear callipers	Steel front discs (rotors) / Steel rear discs (rotors)	Ceramic front discs (rotors) / Ceramic rear discs (rotors)
2.7-litre Boxster and Cayman	Engine-driven vacuum pump	4-piston black / 4-piston black	Vented/cross-drilled / Vented/cross-drilled	N/A
3.2 Boxster S	Engine-driven vacuum pump	4-piston red / 4-piston red	Vented/cross-drilled / Vented/cross-drilled	N/A
3.4-litre Boxster S	Engine-driven vacuum pump	4-piston red / 4-piston red	Vented/cross-drilled / Vented/cross-drilled	N/A
3.4 Cayman S	Engine-driven vacuum pump	4-piston red / 4-piston red	Vented/cross-drilled / Vented/cross-drilled	
Option PCCB*	Engine-driven vacuum pump	6-piston yellow / 4-piston yellow	N/A	Vented/cross-drilled / Vented/cross-drilled

*Porsche Ceramic Composite Brakes (PCCB) option was available for various 1st generation 987 models. The option may have be offered or listed as 'standard' on some '987 special edition' models.

987 model dimensions

Model	Length mm (inches)	Width mm(inches) with door mirrors	Standard roof height mm(inches)	Roof height with option PASM mm(inches)
Boxster & Boxster S Model years 2006 and 2007	4329 (170.4)	1801 (70.9) 1937 (76.3)	1295 (51)	1295 (51)
Boxster & Boxster S Model years 2007 to 2009	4329 (170.4)	1801 (70.9) 1937 (76.3)	1292 (50.9)	1282 (50.5)
Cayman & Cayman S	4372 (172.1)	1801 (70.9) 1937 (76.3)	1305 (51.4)	1296 (51)

987 model empty weights

987 model	Weight range* Kg (lb)
2.7-litre Boxster with manual transmission**	1295 to 1410 (2855 to 3109)
2.7-litre Boxster with Tiptronic transmission**	1355 to 1455 (2987 to 3208)
3.2-litre Boxster S with manual transmission	1345 to 1430 (2965 to 3153)
3.2-litre Boxster S with Tiptronic transmission	1385 to 1470 (3053 to 3241)
2.7-litre Boxster with manual transmission	1305 to 1420 (2877 to 3131)
2.7-litre Boxster with Tiptronic transmission	1365 to 1465 (3009 to 3230)
3.4-litre Boxster S with manual transmission	1355 to 1430 (2987 to 3153)
3.4-litre Boxster S with Tiptronic transmission	1385 to 1470 (3075 to 3241)
2.7-litre Cayman with manual transmission	1300 to 1420 (2866 to 3131)
2.7-litre Cayman with Tiptronic transmission	1360 to 1465 (2998 to 3230)
3.4-litre Cayman S with manual transmission	1350 to 1430 (2976 to 3153)
3.4-litre Cayman S with Tiptronic transmission	1390 to 1470 (3064 to 3243)

*Specific delivered car weight is totally option dependent.
**Model years 2005 and 2006 only

Approved tyres

Porsche approved and tested tyres for 987 models range		
Wheel diameter	Brand and type	Porsche N rating
17-inch	Pirelli P-Zero Rosso	N3
	Bridgestone Potenza S-02A	N4
	Continental ContiSportContact2	N2
	Michelin Pilot Sport PS2	N3
	Pirelli Winter W240 Snowsport	N1
18-inch	Pirelli P-Zero Rosso	N3
	Bridgestone Potenza S-02A	N4
	Continental ContiSportContact2	N2
	Michelin Pilot Sport PS2	N3
	Dunlop SP 9090	N0
	Pirelli P-Zero Rosso	N4
	Pirelli Winter W240 Snowsport	N1
19-inch*	Bridgestone Potenza RE050A	N0
	Bridgestone Potenza RE050A	N1
	Goodyear Eagle F1 Asymmetric	N0
	Michelin Pilot Sport PS2	N2
	Pirelli P-Zero	N2

Not all 987 models are approved to be fitted with 19-inch wheels.

The Essential Buyer's Guide™ series ...

Other titles from Veloce Publishing

Porsche 911 – The Definitive History

1963 – 1971

978-1-903706-28-2

1971 – 1977

978-1-903706-32-9

1977 – 1987

978-1-903706-36-7

1987 – 1997

978-1-903706-39-8

1997 – 2004

978-1-904788-42-3

2004 – 2012

978-1-845848-64-4

From technical manuals, to photo books, to autobiographies, Veloce's range of eBooks gives you the same high-quality content, but in a digital format tailored to your favourite e-reader. Whether it's a technical manual, an autobiography, or a factual account of motorsport history, our ever expanding eBook range offers something for everyone.

www.digital.veloce.co.uk

For more info on Veloce titles, visit our website at www.veloce.co.uk
email: info@veloce.co.uk • Tel: +44(0)1305 260068

Other titles from Veloce Publishing

Porsche 993 – King of Porsche
(Streather)
ISBN: 978-1-845849-38-2
Paperback • 28x21cm • £90.00* UK/$150.00* USA
$195.00* CAN • 640 pages • 1300 b&w pictures
If you own, or are buying, a Porsche 993, this is a
must-have book. Covering all aspects of ownership
including buying advice, maintenance, common
problems, tuning, specifications, and much, much, more,
this really is THE essential companion. Get the most from
your 993!

Porsche 996 – Supreme Porsche
(Streather)
ISBN: 978-1-845849-54-2
Paperback • 28x21cm • £90.00* UK/$150.00* USA
$195.00* CAN • 656 pages • 1545 pictures
Everything a 996 owner needs to know, plus a lot more,
is contained within the covers of this book, in which every
known model and version is described. With over 1500
photos and extensive appendices, this fact-packed book
is a must for any 996 owner. Get the most from your 996!

Porsche 997 2004-2012 – Porsche Excellence
(Streather)
ISBN: 978-1-845846-20-6
Paperback • 28x21cm • £70.00* UK/$140.00* USA
$195.00* CAN • 704 pages • 1500 pictures
Describing every 997 model, Porsche 997 Porsche
Excellence contains everything a 997 owner needs, plus
a lot more. Transmissions, engines, and even engine
management software for national variants are included.

For more info on Veloce titles, visit our website at www.veloce.co.uk
email: info@veloce.co.uk • Tel: +44(0)1305 260068
* prices subject to change, p&p extra

Index